Girolamo Savonarola, F. C. Cowper

An Exposition of the Psalm Miserere Mei Deus

Girolamo Savonarola, F. C. Cowper

An Exposition of the Psalm Miserere Mei Deus

ISBN/EAN: 9783744777605

Printed in Europe, USA, Canada, Australia, Japan

Cover: Foto ©Lupo / pixelio.de

More available books at **www.hansebooks.com**

AN EXPOSITION

—OF—

THE PSALM MISERERE MEI DEUS,

—BY—

FRA GIROLAMO SAVONAROLA.

Written during the imprisonment which preceded his martyr-
dom, in the year of Our Lord, 1498.

TRANSLATED FROM THE LATIN BY

THE REV. F. C. COWPER, B. D.

*"Fac me sicut unum de infantibus et lactentibus tuis: ut semper pen-
deam ab uberibus sapientiæ tuæ."*

MILWAUKEE, WIS.:
THE YOUNG CHURCHMAN CO.,
1889.

PREFACE.

By the Translator.

In recent years, the reading public has taken a decided interest in the history of Florence, and in those worthies who, individually, did their part in making a name and a glory for that deservedly famous city.

The general interest is, however, mostly centered in the group of men who lived in Florence at about the end of the fifteenth century, an epoch marked by the revival of letters, which Lorenzo, the Magnificent, did so much to foster and encourage.

For myself, I freely confess, that among the men who lived, suffered, and died in that stirring period, not one has attracted my own heart and mind with such a constraint, as the famous monk and reformer, FRA GIROLAMO SAVONAROLA, who entered into an unequal contest with a wicked Pope, and who perished in the cause of pure religion.

Grimm, in his "Life of Michael Angelo," George Eliot, in "Romola," Mrs, Oliphant, in "Makers of Florence," and the Century Magazine, issue of August, 1880, gave to the world faithful sketches of the great and good priest of Florence. It is no part of my present purpose to add anything to the story of his life, nor to repeat what has been said by others.

I long desired to obtain a copy of SAVONAROLA's "Triumph of the Cross." In my quest I was happy enough to secure, through the indefatigable efforts of a brother, who chanced to be in London, a very ancient copy of SAVANAROLA's Latin works in one volume. This book bears several dates, the earliest 1511, A. D.; the last, 1523, A. D. It was issued from a Parisian press. This edition, I fancy, is unknown to history, since the only mention I can discover of any addition of SAVONAROLA's works is referred to the first half of the seventeenth century.

Moreover, no translation of our author's works, nor of any part of them, has ever been made into English. Consequently, I am persuaded, that to publish any literary work of considerable merit, from the pen of the Florentine monk, will be not inopportune at this time—nay, that many admirers of his will hail the same with pleasure.

To such, therefore, and to those who love the perusal of pages which express the deeper yearnings of the devout religious soul, I send forth this little volume as a kind of first fruits of the larger task which I have set before me, the translation and publication of the *"Triumphus Crucis."*

FRED. C. COWPER.

AN EXPOSITION OF PSALM LI.,

WRITTEN DURING HIS IMPRISONMENT, BY THE REVEREND
FATHER, BROTHER HIEROME SAVONAROLA, OF
FERRARA, OF THE ORDER OF PREACHERS.

Woe is me, who am destitute of all aid ! Who have offended both heaven and earth ! Whither shall I go ? Whither shall I turn ? To whom shall I flee for refuge ? Who will take pity on me ?

To heaven I dare not lift mine eyes, for I have grievously sinned against it. On earth I cannot find a refuge, for I have been a by-word unto it.

What then shall I do ? Shall I yield to despair ? Away with the thought ! God is merciful. Righteous is my Saviour. Therefore God alone is my refuge.

He will not despise the work of His own hand. He will not cast from Him the image of Himself. To Thee, therefore, most righteous God, disconsolate and full of woe, I come, since Thou alone art my hope, Thou alone art my refuge. But how shall I open my mouth before Thee, when I dare not lift up mine eyes? Shall I pour forth words of lamentation? I will implore Thy mercy. I will say :—

I.

"Have mercy upon me, O God, according to Thy great mercy."

O God! Who dwellest in the inaccessible light! O God! Who hidest Thyself, Who canst not be seen with the carnal eye, nor comprehended by the mind of the creature, nor described in the language of men (or of angels); O, my God! Thee, the incomprehensible, I seek; Thee, the unspeakable, I invoke, whatever Thou art, Who art in every place.

I know, indeed, that Thou art the Supreme Being. If, then, Thou art Being Itself, and not exclusively the cause of all being, and yet withal the Cause—somewhere I shall find the Name by which I seek to address Thy unspeakable Majesty.

Thou art God, say I, Who art whatsoever is in Thee. For Thou art Thy wisdom itself, Thine Excellency, Thy Power, Thy Supreme Felicity.

Since, then, Thou art merciful, what art Thou but Mercy itself? And what am I but Misery itself?

Behold, therefore, O Mercy, O God! behold Misery standing before Thy face. What wilt

Thou do, O Mercy ? Surely Thou wilt perform
Thy work. It is not possible, is it, for Thee to
act against Thy attributes ?

And what is Thy work ? To do away with
misery, to lift up men sunken in wretchedness.
Then have mercy upon me, O God ! O God ! nay,
O Mercy ! take away my wretchedness, take
away my sins, which are now my sum of wretchedness. Lift me up who am in misery. Show
forth in me Thy work. Exercise upon me Thy
virtue.

Deep calleth unto deep. The deep of misery
calleth unto the deep of mercy. The deep of
transgressions calleth unto the deep of grace.
Greater is the deep of mercy than the deep of
misery. Therefore let deep swallow deep. Let
the deep of mercy swallow up the deep of misery.

Have mercy upon me, O God, according to
Thy great mercy, not according to man's mercy,
which is small ; but according to Thine, which is
great, which is immeasurable, which is incomprehensible, which exceedeth the measure of all
transgressions ; according to that Thy great
mercy, by which Thou so lovedst the world, that
Thou gavest Thine only-begotten Son.

What greater mercy can there be ? What
greater love ? Who can yield to despair ? Who

can refuse to have confidence? God was made Man; and for men was crucified. Have mercy upon me, therefore, O God, according to this Thy mercy. By which Thy Son gave Himself for us. By which, through the same, Thou hast taken away the sins of the world. By which, through His cross, Thou hast illumined all men. By which, through the Same, Thou hast renewed the things which are in heaven, and the things which are in earth. Wash me, O Lord, in His blood. Enlighten me in His humility. Renew me by His resurrection.

Have mercy upon me, O God. Not according to a small measure of Thy mercy. For this is the small measure of Thy mercy, when Thou deliverest men from their bodily woes.

But thy mercy is great when Thou dost take away their sins, and when, through Thy grace, Thou liftest men above the heights of earth. Therefore, O Lord, have mercy upon me according to this Thy great mercy, and turn me unto Thee, that Thou mayest make an end of my sins, that Thou mayest justify me through Thy grace.

II.

" And according to the multitude of Thy com-
passions do away mine iniquity."

Thy mercy, O Lord, is the fulness of Thy
holiness, by which Thou regardest the wretched
righteously. For Thy compassions are the works
and the outgoings of Thy mercy.

There came Mary Magdalene to Thy feet,
O blessed Jesus! She washed them with her tears;
she wiped them with her hairs; and Thou didst
pardon her and send her forth in peace. Here
was one of Thy compassions, Lord.

Peter denied, and with an oath blasphemed
Thee. Thou lookedst back upon him. He wept
bitterly, and Thou forgavest him, and didst confirm him chief of the Apostles. This again is
Thy compassion, Lord.

The thief upon the cross was redeemed with
but a single word. Paul, in the heat of persecution, being called, was straightway filled with the
Holy Ghost. These are Thy compassions, Lord.
The time would fail me did I desire to give
account of all thy compassions.

Wherein, verily, was *their* righteousness, the objects of so many compassions?

No man may glory in himself. Let all the just appear, whether in heaven or upon the earth, and we will question them before Thy presence. Was it by their own virtue that they were saved? Surely, every one of them, with one heart, with one mouth must give reply—"Not unto us, O Lord, not unto us; but unto Thy name give the praise; for Thy mercy and Thy truth's sake."

For not through their own sword have they possessed the earth; and it was not their own arm which saved them: but Thy right hand, and Thy arm; and the light of Thy countenance; because Thou hadst a favour unto them. Whence, not by their own merits; not by works were they saved, lest any man should boast; but because so it seemed good in Thy sight. As also the prophet spake, when he wrote concerning himself, saying: He hath saved me, because He had a desire unto me.

Since, then, Thou art the same God, in Whom is no variableness, neither shadow of turning; and we are Thy creatures, as our fathers were, who, through concupiscence were born in sin, as also we ourselves; and there is one Mediator between God and men, Christ Jesus, Who abideth

forever; why pourest Thou not forth Thy compassions upon us, in like manner as Thou didst
pour them forth upon our fathers ?

Hast Thou forgotten us ? Are we alone trans-
gressors ? Was not Christ put to death for us ?
Does Thy mercy no more superabound ?

O Lord, our God, I pray Thee, I beseech Thee,
do away mine iniquity according to the multitude
of Thy compassions. For Thy mercies are many
and infinite. One of them is sufficient for me,
manifestly, that Thou mayest destroy mine
iniquity according to the multitude of Thy compassions : that, as Thou hast drawn to Thyself,
lifted up, and justified countless sinners, Thou
mayest deign to draw to Thyself, lift up, justify
me through Thy grace.

Therefore, according to the multitude of Thy
compassions, do away mine iniquity; break my
heart in pieces, that, all its sin and all its un-
cleanness cast out, it may become like a scoured
tablet, upon which the finger of God may write
the law of His love, in the presence of which no
iniquity may find a dwelling place.

III.

" Wash me throughly from my iniquity: and cleanse me from my sins."

I confess, O Lord, that once Thou hast put away mine iniquity. A second time hast Thou put it away. Thou hast washed me a thousand times.

Wash me again from mine iniquity, because again have I fallen. Shalt Thou place on erring man a definite number to his sins? Thou Who, to Peter's question—How oft shall my brother sin against me and I forgive him? till seven times?—repliedst, I say not unto thee till seven times, but unto seventy times seven, using a limited number to denote an unlimited. Shalt Thou, then, be surpassed in forgiveness by a man? Is not God greater than a man? Is He not better than a man? Rather, is not God the Mighty Lord, and the Upholder of the universe?

Every man living is feeble. God alone is good. But every man is deceitful.

Hast Thou not said, Whensoever a sinner shall repent, I will remember the sum of his iniquities no more?

Behold ! I am a sinner. I repent in anguish. For my wounds are corrupt by reason of my foolishness. I am troubled. I am bowed down even to extremity. All the day long I go mourning unto Thee. I am afflicted and I am humbled ; yea, I have roared through the anguish of my heart.

O Lord, all my longing is before Thee, and my groaning is not hid from Thee. My heart is disquieted within me ; my strength hath left me, and the very light of mine eyes is gone from me.

Why, therefore, O Lord, dost Thou not do away mine iniquity ? And if Thou hast already put it away, according to the multitude of Thy compassions wash me *thoroughly* from my sin ; for hitherto I have been cleansed imperfectly. Complete Thy work. Take away the whole body of sin. Take away the guilt. Increase the light. Inflame my heart with Thy love. Drive away fear ; for perfect love casteth out fear. Let the love of the world, the love of the flesh, the love of glory, and self-love, wholly depart from me.

Thoroughly (and more and more), shalt Thou wash me from mine iniquity wherein I have sinned against my neighbor ; and from my sin wherewith I have offended against God.

Wash me, that Thou mayest take away, not

the crime and the guilt alone, but likewise the fuel of sins.

Thou shalt wash me, verily, with the water of Thy manifold grace; with the water whereof whosoever shall drink, shall never thirst; but it shall be in him a well of water springing up into everlasting life.

Wash me with the water of my tears.

Wash me with the water of Thy Scriptures, that I may be worthy to be numbered among those to whom Thou hast already said, Ye are clean according to My word.

IV.

"For I acknowledge my iniquity, and my sin is ever before me."

Truly, with whatever intention of Thy mercy and Thy compassions, O Lord, I confidently flee to Thee for refuge. Yet I come not as the Pharisee, who, holy in his own eyes, made his prayer; nay, rather made boast of himself, and despised his neighbor; but as the publican, who dared not so much as lift his eyes to heaven, for I acknowledge my iniquity.

For when I think upon my sins, I dare not lift my eyes on high. But, with the publican, in humility, I say, God be merciful to me a sinner. For my soul swayeth betwixt hope and fear. And at one moment, through dread of the sins which I acknowledge to be within me, I despair. At another I am sustained with the hope of Thy mercy.

Verily, because Thy mercy is greater than my misery, my hope shall ever be in Thee, O Lord; and I will sing of Thy compassions for ever and ever.

For I know that Thou desirest not the death

of a sinner; but that he should be converted; but that he should acknowledge his iniquity; but that he should discard his sin, and come to Thee, and live.

O my God! grant unto me that I may live for Thee. For I acknowledge my iniquity. I know how deep it is, how multiform, and how pernicious. I do not ignore it. I do not conceal it. But I set it fast before my eyes, that I may wash it with tears; that I may confess to the Lord my wrong-doing, to my own dispraise. For my sin (wherein I have dealt haughtily against Thee), is ever before me.

Before me, on this account, because I have sinned against Thee. Verily before me; because I have sinned against my own soul; because it ever accuseth me before the Judge; because it condemneth me on every side; and so much the more before me, that it may always stand in my presence opposing itself to me, lest my prayer should pass over unto Thee; that it may take away from me Thy mercy; to hinder it that it should not be able to cross over unto me. Therefore I tremble; therefore I groan; therefore I beseech Thy mercy.

As then, O Lord, Thou has granted unto me to acknowledge my transgression, and to be sorry for my sin, so also make perfect my contrition, make complete my confession, draw to an end my penance. For every good gift, and every perfect gift is from above, and cometh down from Thee, the Father of lights.

V.

" Against Thee only have I sinned, and done evil in Thy sight: that Thou mightest be justified in Thy sayings, and vanquish when Thou art judged."

Against Thee only have I sinned greatly; because Thou taughtest me to love Thee for Thine own sake; to resign the love of created things to Thee. But I have loved the creature more than Thee; loving it for its own sake.

But what is it to sin, except to cling to the creature in love for its own sake? And what is this but to proceed against Thee? Surely, he who loveth the creature for its own sake, maketh the creature his god. I therefore have sinned against Thee only, because I have set up the creature as my god. I have consequently cast Thee away, and done despite against Thee only. For I have not sinned against any one creature, if I have set my aim upon a created thing; because it was not taught me that I should love any one creature for its own sake. For if Thou hadst commanded me to love alone an angel for himself; and I should have set my heart upon money, without doubt I had sinned against the angel. But since Thou alone art to be loved for Thyself, and the creature is to be loved in Thee and for Thee ; verily, against Thee only have I sinned, since I have loved the creature for itself.

But, what is worse, I have done evil in Thy sight. For I have not blushed to sin before Thy face.

O God ! how many sins have I committed in Thy sight, which I would in no wise have perpetrated in the sight of men ! nay, which I could by no means have desired that men should know !

I have stood in awe of men, rather than of Thee ; because I was blind, and loved my blindness. Yea, rather, I neither saw Thee, nor gave heed. I had only carnal eyes. Therefore men alone, who are flesh, did I perceive, and them I feared. But Thou observedst all my sins, and kept account of them. I shall not therefore be able to hide them from Thee, nor evade them, nor flee from Thy presence.

Whither shall I go from Thy spirit ? and whither shall I flee from Thy presence ? What then shall I do ? Whither shall I turn ?

Whom shall I find as the defender whom I long for ? unless it be Thou, O my God ?

Who so good ? Who so tender ? Who so merciful as Thou, that in tenderness surpassest all creatures beyond comprehension ? For it is Thy attribute to pity and to spare ; Who showest forth Thy omnipotence chiefly in sparing and pitying.

I confess, O Lord, that against Thee only have I sinned and done evil in Thy sight.

Have mercy upon me, and show forth Thy omnipotence upon me that Thou mayest be justified in Thy sayings. For Thou saidst, I came not to call the righteous, but sinners to repentance.

Be Thou justified in Thy sayings, O Lord. Call me. Support me. Grant unto me to bring forth fruit meet for repentance. For this cause wast Thou crucified. For this Thou didst die, and wast buried.

Thou saidst also, when I shall have been lifted up from the earth, I will draw all things unto Myself.

Be Thou justified in Thy sayings. Draw me after Thee. We will run in the fragrance of Thy ointments.

Again Thou saidst, Come unto Me, all ye who labor, and are heavy laden, and I will refresh you.

Behold ! I come to Thee heavy laden with sins, laboring day and night in the anguish of my heart.

Refresh me, O Lord, that Thou mayest be justified in Thy sayings, and, that Thou mayest vanquish when Thou art judged.

For there be many that say, There is no help for him in his God; God hath forsaken him. Vanquish these men, O Lord, since Thou art judged by them. Forsake me not utterly. Grant unto me mercy and help, and they are vanquished.

For they say both that Thou wilt not have mercy on me, and that Thou wilt cast me away from Thy presence; because Thou wilt support me no more.

Thus art Thou judged by men.

. Thus do men speak concerning Thee.

These are their judgments. But Thou art tender, and Thou art merciful. Have mercy upon me, and vanquish their judgments. Show forth in me Thy mercy. Let Thy tenderness be magnified in me. Make me one of the vessels of Thy mercy. That Thou mayest be justified in Thy sayings, and vanquish when Thou art judged.

For men judge of Thee as stern and harsh. Vanquish their judgment by Thy tenderness and loving kindness, that men may learn to be merciful to sinners, and that offenders may be roused to penitence, when they behold in me Thy tenderness and loving kindness.

VI.

"For I was begotten in iniquities ; and in sins
hath my mother conceived me."

Regard not, O Lord, the gravity of my sins,
neither consider their multitude ; but take knowledge of Thy framework.

Remember that I am but dust, and that all
flesh is grass.

For behold, I was begotten in iniquities, and
in sins hath my mother conceived me.

My mother, the carnal, I say, hath conceived
me through concupiscence, and therein have I
contracted original sin. Furthermore what is
original sin, except the deprivation of the original righteousness and rectitude of the whole
man ?

Thus it is a man is conceived and born in
human sin. The whole man is wrong. The
whole man is crooked. The flesh lusteth against
the spirit. The reason is weak. The will is
feeble.

Man is frail and like unto vanity. His senses
deceive him. His imagination beguileth him.
His ignorance leadeth him astray. He encounter-

eth infinite obstacles, which draw him back
from the good, and drive him towards the evil.

Therefore is original sin the root of all sins.
It is the touchwood of all iniquities. For, in
whatsoever man you please, owing to his very
nature, there may be just one sin; yet, through
its own strength, it becometh all sins combined.

Thou seest then, O Lord, what I am, and
whence I am. For I was begotten in original
sin, which contains all iniquities, and all transgressions; and in it hath my mother conceived
me. I was altogether born in sins. And, com-
passed about with toils on every side, whither
can I escape?

For I do not the good that I would; but the
evil which I would not, that I do; for I find
another law in my members, warring against the
law of my mind, and bringing me into captivity
to the law of sin and death.

Therefore, by so much the more let Thy
tenderness lift me up, the more frail and com-
passed about with toils it seeth me.

For who doth not pity the feeble? Who
doth not feel for the weak?

Come! O come! Thou Good Samaritan, and
lift me up, who am wounded and half dead; heal
my wounds, and pour in oil and wine; set me

upon Thine own beast; bring me to an inn; commend me to the host; hand him two denarii, and say unto him—Whatsoever thou spendest more, when I come again, I will repay thee.

VII.

"For, behold, thou hast loved truth; and hast shewn unto me the undetermined and hidden things of thy wisdom."

Come! O Sweetest Samaritan! For, behold, Thou hast loved truth. The truth, I say, of the promises which Thou hast made to the human race.

These hast Thou loved exceedingly; because Thou madest them, and hast kept them. For it is Thy very attribute to love; to do good within Thine own self; for Thou art immutable.

Nor thus only dost Thou love us. Thou dost not love only that the deeds of Thy love may pass and repass. But Thou art the absolute love, which never changeth.

For God is love. It is Thine, therefore, to love the creature; to do good unto it. And Thou doest most for those whom Thou lovest most.

What, therefore, is it for Thee to love the truth, except to do and to keep the truth?

Thou promisedst unto Abraham a son, when he was already old, and Sara, barren and stricken in years. Thou didst keep the promise—because Thou lovedst the truth.

Thou didst pledge to the children of Israel a land flowing with milk and honey : and at length Thou gavest it, because Thou lovedst the truth.

Thou didst promise unto David, saying, Of the fruit of thy body will I set upon Thy throne. It was fulfilled, because Thou lovedst the truth.

Countless have been Thy promises, in which Thou hast always been faithful. Wherefore hast Thou always been faithful ? Because Thou lovedst the truth.

Unto sinners fleeing to Thee for refuge, Thou hast promised pardon and grace ; and Thou hast never defrauded any one, because Thou lovedst the truth.

That Prodigal Son, who departed into a far country, and wasted all his substance in riotous living, on returning to himself, came to Thee, saying, Father, I have sinned against heaven and before Thee ; I am no more worthy to be called Thy son ; make me as one of Thy hired servants. When as yet he was a great way off, Thou discernedst him with the eyes of Thy tenderness ; Thou didst run to meet him ; Thou didst fall upon his neck and kiss him ; Thou broughtest forth the best robe ; Thou didst put a ring on his finger, and shoes on his feet ; and killedst the fatted calf ; Thou causedst the whole household to make

merry, saying, Let us make merry and feast; for
this My son was dead, and is alive again: he was
lost, and is found.

Wherefore didst Thou these things, O Lord
God? Without doubt because Thou lovedst the
truth.

Love therefore, Father of mercies, this truth
in me, who am returning to Thee from a far
country. Run to meet me, and give to me the
kiss of Thy lips; bestow the best adornments;
lead me into Thy house; and kill the fatted calf,
that all who hope in Thee may rejoice in me; and
we will feast together at the espousal banquet.

Not, O Lord, for me alone wilt thou preserve
this truth. If Thou, Lord, wilt be extreme to
mark what is done amiss, O Lord, who shall abide
it?

Verily, Thou wilt not be extreme to mark
iniquities; because Thou lovedst the truth. Yea,
Thou hast loved it with an unmeasurable love.
For who is the truth which Thou hast loved, but
Thy Son—Who said, I am the Way, the Truth,
and the Life? For He Himself is the Truth, of
Whom every truth in heaven and in earth is named.

This therefore hast Thou lovèd; and in this
alone wast Thou well pleased; because this alone

Thou didst find without spot, and didst will that it should die for sinners.

Preserve therefore, O God, this truth.

Behold, I am a great sinner, in whom Thou mayest preserve it; to whom Thou mayest pardon many sins, which Thou canst wash away in the blood of Thy Christ, which Thou canst purchase through His passion.

Why, O Lord, didst Thou give to me this conception of Thy Son? Why didst Thou give this faith concerning Him?

Was it that I might be affected with the greater pain, beholding my redemption, and Thou not touch it in the least?

God forbid. But it was that, knowing myself to be prepared, I might come and lay hold of that grace through Christ.

Redeem me then, O Lord, for Thou hast shewn unto me the undetermined and hidden things of Thy wisdom, that this very knowledge might aid me, and lead me unto salvation. These things, of a truth, the philosophers understood not. These things were to them undetermined. These things were wholly hidden unto them. None among men, except a few whom Thou didst love, had knowledge of these things, prior to the Incarnation of Thy Son.

The most inquisitive searchers of the heart ; the wisest men, I say, of this era, lifted up their eyes across the age, and were unable to find out this Thy wisdom ; because Thou hast hid these things from the wise and prudent, and hast revealed them unto babes, even unto humble fishermen, and unto Thy holy prophets, who have handed them down to us.

If, therefore, Thou hast shewn unto me the undetermined and hidden things of Thy wisdom and of Thy Scripture, why do I know them in vain ? For surely it is in vain that I know them if they do not lead me unto salvation. " Because that, when in this wise they had known God ; they did not glorify Him as God, neither were thankful, but became vain in their imaginations. For professing themselves to be wise, they became fools."

Wilt Thou suffer me to be in the number of these ? God forbid. For Thou art the same Mercy which never faileth the penitent.

Spare then, O Lord, spare Thy servant, and confirm him in the number of Thy children ; that the undetermined and hidden things of Thy wisdom, which Thou hast shewn unto him, may lead him to the fountain of wisdom, which is in the highest ; that Thou mayest be praised in Thy work of mercy which Thou shalt perform upon Thy slave, O Lord, Who never failest him that hopeth in Thee.

VIII.

"Thou shalt sprinkle me, O Lord, with hyssop, and I shall be clean: Thou shalt wash me, and I shall be whiter than snow."

Because, O Lord, Thou hast loved truth, and hast shewn unto me the undetermined and hidden things of Thy wisdom, I have conceived a great hope; and I have faith that Thou wilt not cast me away from Thy presence.

Sprinkle me with hyssop, and I shall be clean.

Hyssop is an herb, humble, pungent, and aromatic.

What else does it symbolize except Thy Son, our Lord, Jesus Christ?

Who humbled Himself even unto death, and that the death of the cross.

Who, in the glory of His unmeasured love hath loved us, and washed us from our sins in His own blood.

Who, by the fragrance of His goodness, and meekness, and righteousness, hath filled the whole earth with a sweet savour.

This, then, is the Hyssop wherewith Thou shalt sprinkle me—when Thou shalt pour forth upon me the efficacy of His blood; when Christ shall dwell in me by faith; when, through love, I shall be united to Him; when I shall imitate the humility of His estate.

Then I shall be cleansed from all my impurities.

Then Thou shalt wash me in my tears, shed through love of Christ.

Then I shall travail in my groan; I shall wash my couch every night, and water my bed with my tears.

Then, too, Thou shalt wash me, and I shall be whiter than snow. For snow is dazzling white and cold.

Therefore, if Thou shalt perfectly have sprinkled me with Hyssop, I shall be whiter than snow. For I shall be permeated with Thy supreme brightness, which surpasseth all corporeal splendor. And, through it, being enkindled with the love of heavenly blessings, I shall resign all the dear objects of the flesh ; having become cold toward things terrestial, and set aglow toward things celestial.

IX.

" Thou shalt cause me to hear of joy and gladness; and the bones which have been humbled shall rejoice."

For then, O Lord, will I make my prayer unto thee ; and early in the morning, yea, in the beginning of Thy day, Thou shalt hear my voice.

And I will hear what the Lord God will speak concerning me, when He shall speak peace unto His people.

And Thou shalt give peace unto me, O Lord : peace shalt Thou give unto me, because I have trusted in Thee.

Thou shalt cause me to hear of joy and gladness, when I hear what Mary heard.

And what did Mary hear ?

Of her I speak who wept at Thy feet. What, then, did she hear ? Thy faith hath saved thee ; go in peace.

And I shall hear what the robber heard. This day thou shalt be with Me in Paradise. Therefore I shall have joy for the remission of sins ; gladness for the promise of blessings.

And shall I not rejoice, and shall I not be glad,

when Thou hast granted pardon for all my sins?

Then shall I begin to taste of joy, since Thou art good, O Lord.

Then shall I learn to dwell in heavenly places.

Then shall I say with the prophet. How plentiful is Thy goodness, which Thou hast hid away for them that fear Thee!

Then shall I rejoice and be glad; and the bones which have been humbled shall rejoice.

What are the bones which uphold the flesh, except the forces of the rational soul which support the weak fabric of my body, lest it should flow into all imperfections, lest the entire man should become flesh, and be wholly dissolved?

Therefore these bones have been humbled, because the reason has been greatly enfeebled, and the will vehemently prone to evil.

No longer does the flesh obey the reason, but the reason the flesh. I am unable to resist vice, because my bones have been humbled.

And wherefore were they humbled? Because they have forsaken Thee, the fountain of living waters, and hewed them out of broken cisterns, that can hold no water, because they are not replenished with Thy grace, without which no man can live uprightly. For without Thee we can do nothing.

They trusted in their own virtue, which was not virtue. Therefore they failed, through their own foolishness.

Therefore let Thy virtue, O Lord, draw near, and the bones which have been humbled shall rejoice.

Let Thy grace draw near.

Let faith, which worketh through love, draw near.

Let Thy virtues and Thy blessings draw near, and the bones which have been humbled shall rejoice.

The reason also shall rejoice.

The memory shall be glad.

The will shall have joy.

They shall rejoice exceedingly, because they shall leap out of themselves.

While they shall give themselves unto good works, they shall be stirred by a great virtue within them. Neither shall they fail. But, with Thy aid, they shall continue even unto the end.

X.

"Turn Thy face from my sins, and blot out all mine iniquities."

Why, O Lord, regardest Thou my sins?

Why numberest them?

Why so carefully considerest them?

Is there anything Thou knowest not? Because man is as a flower of the field, why regardest Thou not rather the face of Thy Christ?

Woe is me! Why do I behold Thee incensed against me?

I confess that I have sinned. But do Thou, O benignant One, have mercy upon me. Turn Thy face from my sins. Thy face is Thy knowledge.

Turn therefore Thy knowledge from my sins.

I speak not concerning the knowledge of mere apprehension, because Thou seest all things always; but concerning the knowledge of approval and disapproval; by means of which Thou approvest the deeds of the just, and condemnest unto reprobation the misdeeds of the wicked.

Do not so take knowledge of my sins as to impute them unto me. But turn Thy face from my sins, that they may be blotted out through Thy mercy.

Regard, O Lord, the soul which thou hast created : look upon Thy image which thou hast formed. For thou madest it after Thy likeness.

And I, wretched man that I am, have overlaid it with the image of the devil, that Thou mayest not be angry at me. And look upon Thine own image, that Thou mayest take pity on me.

O merciful Lord, remember that Thou didst look upon Zacchæus, as he climbed into the sycamore tree, and didst enter into his house, which Thou clearly wouldst never have done if Thou hadst beheld in him the image of the Devil. But because Thou sawest Thine image in him Thou hadst compassion on him, and bestowedst upon him salvation.

He promised to restore fourfold his ill-gotten gains and to spend the half of his goods upon the poor, and he obtained mercy and salvation.

I surrender myself wholly unto Thee. I withhold nothing for myself. I promise always to serve Thee with a true heart. I will perform my vows all the days of my life.

Why, therefore, O Lord, dost Thou not behold in me also Thine image ? Why considerest Thou my sins hitherto ? Turn, I beseech Thee,

Thy face from my sins—and Blot Out All Mine Iniquities.

Blot them all out, I say, that not one may remain. For it is written, Whosoever shall keep the whole law, and yet offend in one, he is guilty of all. Therefore he is condemned to Gehenna, which is the punishment of all sins that lead unto death.

Blot out, then, all my iniquities, that not one thing may offend Thee, which can make me guilty of all.

XI.

" Create in me a clean heart, O God, and renew a right spirit in my inward parts."

For my heart hath forsaken me. It never thinketh upon me, being altogether forgetful of its own safety. It wandereth through crooked paths. It has taken its departure away from home. It followeth after vanities, and its eyes are cast into the extremities of the earth. I have called unto it, and it hath not answered me. It hath departed. It hath perished. It hath been sold unto sins.

What then, O Lord, what shall I say ? Create a clean heart in me, O God. An humble heart. A meek heart. A peaceful heart. A benevolent heart. A devout heart. Which doeth evil to no man. Which repayeth not evil for evil ; but, for evil, good. Which loveth Thee above all things ; thinketh always upon Thee ; speaketh concerning Thee ; giveth Thee thanks ; taketh delight in hymns and spiritual songs ; hath its conversation in Heaven.

Create such a heart in me, O God. Evolve it out of nothing ; that, such as it cannot be by na-

ture, such it may become through grace. For this
cometh into the soul from Thee alone, by creation.
This is the form of a clean heart, bringing with
it all virtues, at the same time it driveth out all
vices. Therefore create in me a clean heart, O
God, through Thy grace.

And renew a right spirit in my inward parts.
For Thy Spirit shall lead me into the right way ;
because it will purge me from worldly affections,
and shall uplift me toward the heavenly. For
the loving and the beloved are one. Who, therefore, loveth carnal things is carnal. But whoso
loveth the Spirit is spirit.

Grant unto me a spirit loving Thee, and wor-
shipping Thee, the Supreme Spirit. For God is a
Spirit ; and they who worship Him must worship
Him in spirit and in truth.

Give a right spirit, not one which seeketh its
own things, but the things which are Thine. Renew a right spirit in my inward parts. Renew it,
because the first which Thou gavest to me, my
sins have destroyed. Give a fresh spirit which re-
neweth, which becometh established.

For my soul is spirit ; and by Thee was so
created, that in itself it was just. For by its own
nature it loveth Thee more than itself, and for
Thy sake desireth all things. For natural love is

just, in so far as it is from Thee. But through its depraved will it hath become established in sins, and maketh natural love to pine away.

Renew, therefore, this spirit, and this love, through Thy grace, that it may press on justly, in accordance with its nature.

Renew it in my inward parts, that it may so make fast its roots in Thine, that it never more can be plucked out.

Renew it, I say, in my inward parts, that it may always inflame me with divine love ; may always make me to pant after Thee ; to hold Thee fast and never to forsake Thee.

XII.

"Cast me not away from Thy presence, and take not Thy Holy Spirit from me."

Behold, Lord, I stand before Thy face, that I may obtain Thy mercy.

I stand in the presence of Thy goodness and beneficence. I look for a gracious answer—that Thou wilt not cast me away from Thy presence in confusion.

Whoever, Lord, came to Thee and departed in confusion? Who desired to see Thy face and went away empty? Surely, Thou surpassest, in the abundance of Thy tenderness, both the deserts and the vows of suppliants; and art wont to give more than men either desire or comprehend.

Never hath it been heard that Thou didst drive away from Thy presence in confusion, any one who came to Thee.

Am I, Lord, to be the first cast away from Thy presence? Or dost thou wish, from me, to make a beginning of confounding those who come to Thee? Dost Thou wish no more to pity and to spare? Far be it.

The Canaanitish woman followed after Thee.

She made a clamor. She filled the air with her cries. Thy disciples were moved to compassion. And Thou heldest Thy peace. In agitation, she persevered. She worshipped Thee, saying—Lord, help me. But Thou, not even so, returnedst answer. Thy disciples besought Thee for her, saying, Send her away, for she crieth after us.

What, I pray, O Lord, didst Thou reply to them ? Yea, to her, who vainly wept, who laboured ineffectually ? Verily, Thou saidst, I am not sent but unto the lost sheep of the house of Israel.

When she heard this, what ought the Canaanitish woman to have done ? Surely, to have despaired of the favor she desired. Not even now did she despair ; but, trusting in Thy mercy, again and again she besought Thee, saying, Lord, help me. To whom unceasingly persisting, Thou, Lord, repliedst, It is not good to take the children's bread and to cast it to dogs. As if Thou hadst plainly said, Depart from me. Ye Canaanites are dogs ; ye are unclean ; ye are idolaters. The gifts of celestial grace belong not to you. It is not meet to take these from the Jews, who worship the true God, and to give them to you—dogs, worshippers of demons.

What now wilt Thou do, O woman of Canaan ? Blush now, and depart. For the Lord is angry—not with thee alone, but with the whole of thy people.

Who, O Lord God, pierced through with these Thy words, had not gone away ? Who had not deeply murmured ? Who had not adjudged Thee cruel ?

And yet this woman persevered in prayer. She lost not hope. Hard words she took not ill. She was not angered, but greatly humbled. And persevering in her petition, she said, with confidence, Yea, Lord, Thou speakest truth. But I seek not the bread, I demand not the privileges of the children, for I am a dog. I seek the crumbs which fall from the table of Thy children. They abound in miracles and graces. But to me let not this smallest favour be denied—that my daughter be delivered from a devil; for even the dogs eat of the crumbs which fall from their masters' table.

Behold ! how great faith ! how great trust ! how great humility ! Thou, by no means angry at her importunity, but rejoicing in her virtue, saidst, O woman, great is thy faith ; be it unto thee even as thou wilt.

Why were these things written, O Lord God ? That we may learn to hope in Thee. That we may persevere in prayer, devoutly and humbly.

For Thou willest to give. But the kingdom of
Heaven suffereth violence, and the violent take it
by storm. Whatsoever things were written afore
time were written for our learning, that through
patience and comfort of the Scriptures we might
have hope.

Cast me not away, therefore, from Thy presence. Lord, Who day and night stand weeping and
wailing before Thy face—not to have Thee deliver
me from bodily violence at the hands of devils ;
but to have Thee rescue my soul from his spiritual
power.

Confound me not, good Jesus ! because I hope
in Thee alone.

There is no salvation for me, except in Thee,
O Lord. For all men have forsaken me. Even
my brethren and my sons have cast me off, my inward parts abhor me. I have none to hear me
any more but Thee. Therefore cast me not away
from Thy presence and take not Thy Holy Spirit
from me.

No man can say Lord Jesus but by the Holy
Spirit. Therefore, if I invoke Thee, Lord Jesus,
I do this by the Holy Spirit. If I grieve for sins
committed ; if I seek for pardon, this assuredly I
do by the Holy Spirit. Yea, I pray Thee, take
not Thy Holy Spirit from me, that He may abide

with me, and labor with me. For we know not how to pray as we ought. But the Spirit helpeth our infirmity and intercedeth for us, yea, causeth us to make our petition with groanings unutterable.

Therefore, take not Thy Holy Spirit from me, that He may teach me how to pray ; and may aid me in my travail, and may make me to persevere in prayers and tears, that at length I may find favour in Thy sight, and serve Thee all the days of my life.

XIII.

"Restore unto me the joy of Thy salvation ; and establish me with Thy free Spirit."

I ask a great favour, O Lord. For Thou art God the mighty Lord, and the great King above all gods. He doeth Thee wrong who asketh a small thing of Thee.

All things are small which are transitory. All carnal things are small. The spiritual are great and precious. Take away the spirit, take away the soul from the body, what remaineth but excrement ? what but dust and a shadow ? Therefore there is as wide a difference between the spirit and the body as between the body and its shadow. Who, therefore, asketh of Thee carnal things asketh small things. But whoso demandeth spiritual things, verily demandeth great things. But he who asketh the joy of Thy salvation asketh the greatest of all.

For what is Thy salvation but Jesus, Thy Son ? This is the true God and eternal life.

Why, then, may I not ask of Thee, O infinite and most bountiful Father, this salvation which Thou didst yield up for me upon the cross ?

Thou didst offer Him to me. Wherefore should I blush to ask Him ?

He is the greatest and infinite Gift, and I am not worthy of a Gift so great. Nevertheless it becometh Thee to give such great things. Hence, by reason of this ineffable tenderness, I dare to approach Thee trustingly and to ask the joy of Thy salvation.

For if any son should ask a fish from the father of his flesh, will he offer him a serpent ? And if he should ask an egg, would he give him a scorpion ? And if he should ask bread, will he give him a stone ?

If, therefore, earthly fathers, being evil and sinners, know how to give to their children the good things which have been bestowed on them by Thee, how much more wilt Thou, O heavenly Father, Who art good in Thy very essence, give the Holy Spirit to them that ask Thee.

Behold ! Thy son returned from a far country, grieving and repentant, asketh of Thee a fish of faith ; (for, just as a fish lurketh beneath the waters, so is faith concerning those things which are not seen.) He asketh, I say, a true faith, that he may rejoice in Thy salvation. Wilt Thou offer unto him a serpent ? Wilt Thou give to him the poisons of unbelief which proceed from the tortuous and old serpent, the Devil ?

I ask of Thee, O Lord, an egg of hope. That just as a chicken is hoped for from the egg, so Thou mayest grant unto me to come out of hope unto the actual vision of Thy salvation ; that out of hope itself the vision may come forth, like as the chicken from the egg.

I ask an egg of hope, that my soul may be sustained by very hope in this vale of tears, and may rejoice in Thy salvation.

Wilt Thou give to me a scorpion of despair, that just as a scorpion hath poison in the end of his tail, so also I may reserve sin in the extremity of my life ? and may flatter myself in the allurements of the world, just as a scorpion outwardly seemeth to flatter ?

I ask also of Thee the bread of Christ's charity, by which He communicateth Himself to all as bread, that I may always rejoice in Thy salvation. Wilt Thou give me a stone, which is hardness of heart ? God forbid.

Why therefore shall I hesitate to ask and to demand great things of Thee, O Lord, Who reassurest me and invitest me to the asking and the knocking, even to importunity ? But what can I ask, more pleasing to Thee and more whole-

some for me, than that Thou shouldest restore to
me the joy of Thy salvation ?

I have already tasted how good the Lord is,
how easy and how light is His burden.

I recall how great peace, how great tranquillity
of soul I did enjoy, when I rejoiced in the Lord,
and exulted in God my Jesus. Yea, now I grieve
the more, because I know what I have lost. I
know what very great benefits I have lost. Yea,
I clamor importunately—Restore to me the joy of
Thy salvation: restore what Thou hast taken
away from me on account of my sins : restore
what I have lost through my own fault : restore,
I beseech Thee, through His merits. Who ever
standeth at Thy right hand and maketh interces-
sion for us. That through Him I may feel that
Thou art reconciled to me ; that the seal is
set upon my heart; that I may say with the
Apostle—1 am nailed to the Cross with Christ:
nevertheless I live; yet not I, but Christ liveth
in me.

Verily, because my frailty is great, establish
me with Thy free Spirit that I may, through no
disquietudes, be capable of separation from Christ;
through no terrors, of departing from Thee;
through no tortures, of becoming weak. For

my strength is not such that it can do battle with
the old serpent and prevail against him.

Peter hath instructed me how great is our
infirmity. He beheld Thee, Lord Jesus! He
conversed with Thee on most familiar terms. He
was partaker of Thy glory in the Mount, when
Thou wast transfigured. He heard the voice of
the Father. He saw with his own eyes Thy
wonderful works. He himself, in like manner,
through Thy power, performed many miracles.
He walked over the waters on his feet. He heard
daily Thy words, so great in power, so great in
gentleness. He appeared most fervent of faith.
And he declared that he was ready to go with
Thee both to prison and to death. And when
Thou foretoldest to him his denial, he did not
believe Thee. He trusted in his own strength.
He directed his faith more toward himself, a
man, than toward Thee, God.

But when a maiden said to him—Thou art
one of them—immediately, being terrified, he
denied it. Another maiden came, and said—
Surely thou art one of them. A second time he
denied it. He could not stand before a mere
woman. How could he have stood before kings
and tyrants?

And when again he was questioned and ac-

cused by them that stood by, he began to swear,
and to call to witness that he knew Thee
not. What thinkest Thou he said? I believe he
sware by God, and by the Law of Moses, that he
knew Thee not; and that he uttered an impreca-
tion, saying—Think ye that I am a disciple of
this Samaritan, seducer, and demoniac, Who hath
destroyed our Law? I am a disciple of Moses.
As for this Fellow, I know not whence He is.

Thanks be to God that the questioning ceased.
For if the questioning had not ceased, neither
would the denying have ceased. For a thousand
questions there had been a thousand denials; and,
as a consequence, a thousand perjuries and imprecations.

Moreover, these questions were but words.
How had it been if the Jews had resorted to
scourges? Verily, Peter would have left nothing undone, by means of which, through denials,
and purjuries, imprecations and blasphemies, he
might extricate himself from their hands. But
Thou, tender Lord, didst look back upon him,
and straightway he knew his sin. But not yet
did he dare to spring forth in the midst, and confess Thee to be the Son of God; because not yet
was he established with power from on high.
For I am far from doubting that he would again

have made denial, if he had seen the scourges
made ready for him. Indeed, on maturer thought,
he went forth and wept bitterly. And Thou,
verily, after Thy resurrection, appearedst unto
him and re-assuredst him.

Nevertheless he remained hidden for fear of
the Jews. He saw Thee so gloriously ascending
into heaven. And he was comforted by a vision
of angels. And yet he dared not even now to appear
in public. Experience, in fact had taught him
his frailty, and proved his weakness. He earnestly
awaited the promise of the Holy Ghost. *He* came
and replenished his bosom with grace. Then he
issued forth. Then he began to speak. Then he
bore the testimony of Thy resurrection with great
power. Then he feared not chief priests and
kings, but gloried in tribulations, and embraced
the cross as the sum of delights.

Therefore, O Lord, establish me in Thy free
Spirit, that I may continue fast in the joy of Thy
salvation. Otherwise I am unable to persevere
against so many warfares. The flesh lusteth
against the spirit. The world presseth me on
every side. The devil sleepeth not. Give to me
the power of Thy Spirit, that a thousand may
fall beside me, and ten thousand at my right

hand, that I may be a faithful and strong witness of thy faith.

For if Peter, whom Thou endowedst with so many gifts and graces, fell so miserably, what could I do, O Lord, who have never beheld Thee in the flesh, nor have partaken of Thy glory in the Mount, nor have been eye-witness of Thy miracles? Nay rather, I have with difficulty comprehended Thy wonderful works from afar: and I have never heard Thy voice, but have always abode in sins. Therefore establish me with thy free Spirit, that I may be able to persevere in Thy obedience, and to give my life for Thee.

XIV.

" I will teach Thy ways unto the wicked ; and sinners shall be converted unto Thee."

Ascribe not this to rashness, O Lord, if I desire to teach Thy ways unto the wicked. For, not as iniquitous, infamous, and in bonds, do I desire to teach the wicked. But if Thou shouldest restore to me the joy of Thy salvation; if Thou shouldest establish me with Thy free Spirit; if Thou shouldest deliver me from my woes, then I shall teach Thy ways unto the wicked.

For this is not difficult to Thee ; because, from the stones Thou art able to raise up children unto Abraham. Nor are sins able to obstruct Thee, if Thou desirest to do this. Yea, rather, where sin abounded, grace also superabounded.

Paul, breathing out threatenings and slaughter against the disciples of the Lord, received authority that if he found any, whether they were men or women, following after Thee, and confessing Thy faith, he should bring them bound unto Jerusalem. He went, therefore, borne by rage, as it were a ravening wolf, to scatter, seize and slay Thy sheep. While, therefore, he was on the way ;

in the madness of persecution ; in the act of sin ;
while he was pursuing Thee ; while he sought to
kill Thy sheep ; while there was in him no prep-
aration for grace and no conscience of sins ; when
with all his power he was opposing Thee, blas-
pheming Thee, and cursing Thee, behold the voice
of Thy tenderness above him, saying, Saul, Saul,
why persecutest thou Me ? By which Voice he
was instantly prostrated and attent, prostrated in
body, attent in mind. Thou didst arouse the
slumberer. Into the eyes weighed down with
sleep Thou didst infuse Thy light ; Thou didst
shew Thy face ; Thou didst pour out Thy ineffable
mercy. The dead arose. He opened his eyes. He
beheld Thee and said, Lord, what wouldst Thou
have me to do ?

Thou sentest the wolf to a lamb. Thou sentest
Him to Ananias. He was baptized. And immediately, being filled with the Holy Ghost, he became a chosen vessel to bear Thy name before
Kings, and the Gentiles, and the children of
Israel. Straightway, therefore, entering the syna-
gogues, he boldly preached Thee, declaring that
Thou art the Christ. He disputed with, he pre-
vailed against, he confounded the Jews.

Behold, Lord, how forthwith out of a persecutor Thou madest him a preacher ; and such and

so great a one that he labored more than the other Apostles. O wonderful power of Thine! If Thou willest to make a just man out of a sinner, a preacher out of a persecutor, who shall prevent Thee? who shall resist Thee? who shall be able to say, why doest Thou so? All things whatsoever pleased Thee, hast Thou done in Heaven and in earth; in the sea and in all deeps.

Then impute it not to arrogance if, not in mine own, but in Thy power, I desire to teach Thy ways unto the wicked. For I know that I can present nothing unto Thee which may please the eyes of Thy Holiness more. This sacrifice is the greatest of all. I can also do nothing more beneficial to myself.

If therefore Thou wilt transform me into a new man, I will teach Thy ways unto the wicked. Not the ways of Plato; not of Aristotle; not the perplexities of the logicians; not the dogmas of the philosophers; not the swelling words of the rhetoricians; not the business of the world; not the ways of vanity; not the ways which lead unto death. But Thy ways, and Thy precepts, which lead unto life. Not one of Thy ways only; but many ways, because Thy precepts are many. Nevertheless all these ways terminate in one. For all are united in one through charity, which, verily, uniteth the souls of the faithful, that there may be in them one heart and one mind in the Lord.

As, forsooth, there are divers ways, so there are divers lives. For by one the clergy walk ; by another the monks ; by another the mendicants. Another have those united in marriage. Another those living and restraining themselves in widowhood. Another the virgins. Another princes follow. Another the doctors. Another the merchants. Finally, the various estates of men proceed through various ways toward the celestial Fatherland.

I will teach therefore, Thy ways unto the wicked ; and to each one equally his own condition and estate. And sinners shall be converted unto Thee, because I shall preach to them not my own self, but Christ crucified. Therefore they shall be converted, not to my praises, but to Thee. For they shall abandon their own ways, that, entering into Thine, they may walk in them, and attain unto Thee.

XV.

" Deliver me from bloodguiltiness, O God, Thou
God of my salvation : and my tongu eshall sing
of Thy righteousness."

In a sea of bloodguiltiness I choke ; and out of
its depth I call unto Thee, O Lord ; Lord hear my
voice.   Delay not, O Lord, for I am nigh unto
death ; that is, my blood and my sins are.   For,
just as in the blood is the life of the flesh ; so in sin is
the life of the sinner.   Pour out the blood, the
animal dieth.   Pour out sin, through confession,
he dieth unto sin, and is made just.

I, therefore, am not only involved in blood ;
but, being steeped in bloodguiltiness, the whirl-
pools of blood drag me beneath.   Succour me, O
Lord, lest I perish.

Deliver me from bloodguiltiness, O God, Who
governest and promotest all things ; Who alone
canst deliver me ; in Whose hand is every breath
of life.

Deliver me from bloodguiltiness, O God, the
Author of my salvation : O God in Whom alone
is my health.

Deliver me, O Lord, as Thou deliveredst Noah from the waters of the flood.

Deliver me as Thou deliveredst Lot from the burning of Sodom.

Deliver me as Thou deliveredst the children of Israel from the deep of the Red Sea.

Deliver me as Thou deliveredst Jona out of the whale's belly.

Deliver me as Thou deliveredst the Three Children from the burning fiery furnace.

Deliver me as Thou deliveredst Peter from the peril of the sea.

Deliver me as Thou deliveredst Paul from the abyss of the sea.

Deliver me as Thou hast delivered numberless sinners from the hand of death, and from the gates of hell.

And my tongue shall sing of Thy righteousness thenceforth; especially Thy righteousness which I shall feel within me through Thy grace. For Thy righteousness, as saith the Apostle, is, through the faith in Jesus Christ, in all and over all who believe in Him. Therefore my tongue shall sing, in giving praise for this Thy righteousness, in extolling Thy grace, in magnifying Thy loving-kindness, in confessing my sins. That in me Thy *mercy* may be praised, which condescended

to justify so great a sinner.   That all men
may know Thou savest them that hope in Thee,
and deliverest them from the clutch of anguish,
O Lord, our God.

XVI.

"O Lord, Thou wilt open my lips; and my
mouth shall shew forth Thy praise."

A great thing is Thy praise, O Lord; and it
proceedeth from the fountain, of which the sinner drinketh not. For praise is not fair in the
mouth of a sinner. Deliver me from bloodguiltiness, O God, Who art my God, and the God of my
salvation: and my tongue shall sing of Thy
righteousness. Then, O Lord, Thou wilt open my
lips, and my mouth shall shew forth Thy praise.

For Thou hast the keys of David, who shut-
test, and no man openeth; and who openest and
no man shutteth. Accordingly, open Thou my
lips, as Thou hast opened the lips of babes and
sucklings, out of whose mouth Thou hast perfected Thy praise.

These, of a truth were prophets and apostles,
and Thy other saints beside, who praised Thee
out of a simple and pure heart and mouth: but
not philosophers and orators who said—We will
magnify our own tongues, our lips are our own,
who is our God? They opened their own lips:

Thou didst not open them.   Verily, out of their mouth Thou hast not perfected praise.

Thy babes, O Lord, praise Thee and despise themselves.   The philosophers, while they made a shew of praising Thee, desired to magnify themselves.   Thy sucklings praise Thy glory; they knew Thee through grace which is heavenly. The philosophers knew Thee through nature alone; they could not sound Thy praises perfectly. Thy saints praised Thee in heart and mouth; and in good works.   The philosophers in words only, and in swelling sophistry.

Thy servants shewed forth Thy praises in all the earth.   The philosophers preached to but a few disciples.   Thy friends, by Thy praises, turned countless men from sin to virtue and true happiness.   The philosophers knew not either true virtue or true happiness.   Thy beloved preached Thy ineffable loving-kindness, which Thou didst manifest in the Son of Thy love. The philosophers could in no wise comprehend this.   Therefore, out of the mouth of babes and sucklings hast Thou perfected Thy praise.

For it hath ever pleased Thee to exalt the humble, and to abase the proud.   Since, then, Thou dost always resist the proud, give unto me true humility, that out of my mouth Thou mayest perfect Thy praise. Give unto me the heart of a little child ; because, except I be converted and become as a little child, I cannot enter into the kingdom of heaven.

Make me as one of Thy babes and sucklings, that I may always hang upon the breast of Thy wisdom. For its breasts are better than wine. And better is wisdom than all riches beside. And all things which are desirable are not worthy to be compared with it. For it is an inexhaustible treasure unto men ; and they who use it are made partakers of the friendship of God.

If therefore Thou makest me a little child, Thou wilt perfect Thy praise in my mouth. For then Thou wilt open my lips ; and my mouth shall shew forth Thy praise. It shall shew it forth, indeed, to perfection, after the manner Thou hast perfected praise out of the mouths of babes and sucklings.

XVII.

*"For if Thou hadst desired a sacrifice, I would
have given it: but Thou wilt not take delight
in burnt offerings."*

My mouth, O Lord, shall shew forth Thy
praise : for I know that this is most acceptable
unto Thee. For Thou sayest by the prophet,
The sacrifice of praise shall honour me ; to him
who walketh in this path I will shew my salvation. I will therefore offer praise to Thee, the
praise that is, of babes and sucklings, for all my
sins.

And why shall I offer unto Thee, for all my
sins, praise rather than sacrifice ? Because, if
Thou hadst desired a sacrifice, I would have given
it : but Thou wilt not take delight in burnt offerings.

Canst Thou be appeased with blood of goats or
of calves ? Wilt Thou eat bull's flesh ? or drink
the blood of goats ? or, peradventure, dost Thou
require gold, Who art the possessor of heaven and
earth ? Dost Thou not desire that a sinner
should be converted and live ?

Notwithstanding, I will chastise my flesh in

due proportion, that, through Thy grace, it may be subjected unto reason, and may faithfully serve it. For if, in this thing, I should exceed the due proportion, it would be accounted to me for sin, that the reason (as saith Thine Apostle) may be obedient unto the truth.

For Thou hast said by the prophet, I will have mercy and not sacrifice. Therefore my mouth shall shew forth Thy praise; for this oblation honoureth Thee, and layeth open to us the way of Thy salvation.

My heart is ready, O God : my heart is ready ; ready through Thy grace for all things which are pleasing to Thee to be done. This one thing have I found most acceptable unto Thee. This I offer unto Thee. This shall ever be in my heart. This my lips shall sound forth.

For if Thou hadst desired a bodily sacrifice, I surely would have given it. For my heart is ready, through Thy grace, to fulfil Thy will. But, on this wise, Thou wilt not take delight in burnt offerings. For Thou didst create bodies for spirits ; therefore Thou seekest spiritual things— not corporeal. For Thou sayest in a certain place, My son, give Me thine heart. This is the sacrifice which pleaseth Thee—that a heart be offered unto Thee, awakened to sorrow for sins, and enkindled with love for heavenly blessings. And it need be repeated no more that Thou *wilt* take delight in this kind of sacrifice.

XVIII.

"The sacrifice of God is a troubled spirit; a contrite and humble heart, O God, Thou wilt not despise."

Verily, a troubled spirit, not a troubled flesh, pleaseth Thee. For the flesh is troubled because it hateth earthly pains, which it desireth not to have, or truly, which it feels within itself. But the spirit is made sad for the fault within, which is contrary to God, Whom it loves. It grieves to have offended its Creator and Redeemer; to have despised His blood so efficacious; to have held the good Father in contempt.

This then—a troubled spirit—is a sacrifice to Thee of a most sweet-smelling savour; for it is composed of very bitter aromatics, that is, of the memory of sins. For when its sins are drawn together in the mortar of the heart; and are crushed with the pestle of compunction, and reduced to powder; and are moistened with water of tears; then it becometh an ointment and a sacrifice most acceptable to Thee; the which oblation Thou wilt in no wise despise.

Who, therefore, breaketh and bruiseth his own

stony heart, made of the adamantine stones of
sin, whence an unguent may be compounded
with the abundance of tears ; and humbly offer-
eth unto Thee this kind of sacrifice, despairing
not at all for the multitude or the gravity of his
sins, will by no means be despised by Thee : because a contrite and humbled heart, O God, Thou
wilt not despise.

Mary Magdalene, who was a sinner in the city,
composed such an ointment. She placed it in the
alabaster box of her heart. She feared not to
enter the house of the Pharisee. Moreover, she
cast herself down at Thy feet. She blushed not
to weep in the midst of the banquet. Oppressed
with sorrow, she spoke not a word ; but her heart
was melted in tears, with which she washed Thy
feet. With her hairs she wiped them. She an-
ointed them with ointment, and ceased not to
kiss them.

Who ever heard of such a thing ? Or who hath
seen anything like this ? Acceptable, therefore,
unto Thee was this her sacrifice ; and, indeed, so
pleasing, that Thou didst prefer her to the
Pharisee, who appeared just unto himself. For,
by Thy words, Thou impliedst that there was as
wide a difference between the justification of Mary
and the righteousness of the Pharisee as was the

difference between washing the feet with water
and bathing them with tears ; kissing the face
once, and kissing the feet unceasingly ; anointing the head with oil, and anointing the feet with
very precious ointment. Yea, rather, that Mary
very far surpassed the Pharisee, because he himself had given Thee neither water, nor kiss, nor oil.

Oh, great virtue of Thine, Lord ! Oh, great
power of Thine ! which manifesteth itself in sparing and pitying !

Behold, therefore ; because a contrite and
humbled heart, O God, thou wilt not despise, on
this account I am eager to make to Thee an offering of this kind. Neither is it needful for me to
plead this with words. For Thou art God, Who
searchest the reins and hearts. Then also receive
this my sacrifice.

And if peradventure it is imperfect, do Thou,
Who alone canst, make it perfect : that it may
become a burnt sacrifice, as it were wholly aglow
with the fire of Thy boundless love : that it may
be acceptable to Thee ; or at the least, that Thou
mayest not despise it.

For if Thou wilt not despise it, I know that I
shall find favour in Thy sight. And after this,
none of Thy saints, whether in heaven or in earth,
will despise me.

XIX.

" Do favourably, O Lord, in Thy good pleasure,
unto Zion : that the walls of Jerusalem may
be builded."

For because it is written, With the holy thou
shalt be holy ; and with an innocent man thou
shalt be innocent ; and with the elect, thou shalt
be elected ; and with the perverse, thou shalt be
perverted. I earnestly desire that all men should
be saved, and come to the knowledge of the truth.
For this is both needful unto them, and expedient
unto me. For, through their prayers, their merits, and their examples, I should arise again, and
be provoked daily to better things.

I beseech Thee, therefore, O Lord, as a sinner,
Do favourably in Thy good pleasure unto Zion ;
that the walls of Jerusalem may be builded. For
I know Thy Church. For Zion is interpreted
watch tower ; because Thy Church, by the grace of
the Holy Ghost, gazeth upon the glory of God, at
the entrance of this road. As the Apostle accordingly said, We, with open face beholding the
glory of the Lord, are changed into the same

image, from glory to glory, as by the Spirit of the Lord.

O Lord God, how small is Thy Church to-day! Already the whole world perisheth. For a great many more are the infidels than the Christians.

Moreover, among the Christians, where are they, who having forsaken worldly aims, look for the glory of the Lord? Surely Thou shalt find few, in comparison with those who savour of earthly things; whose god is their belly, and whose glory is in their shame.

Do favourably, O Lord, in Thy good pleasure unto Zion; that she may be increased in worthiness and in number.

Look down from heaven and do favourably, according as Thou art wont; that Thou mayest send forth upon us from above the fire of Thy love, to consume all our sins. Act, O Lord, in Thy good pleasure; that Thou mayest not deal with us according to our sins, neither reward us according to our iniquities. But deal Thou with us according to Thy great mercy.

Thou, Lord, art our Father, and our Redeemer; Thou art our Peace and our Joy; Thou art our Hope and our eternal Safety. All creatures expect good from Thee. When Thou givest to them, they gather. When Thou openest Thy hand, all things are filled with goodness. When Thou turnest away Thy face, they are troubled. Thou takest away their breath, and they die and return unto their dust. Thou sendest forth Thy Spirit, and they are created : and Thou shalt renew the face of the earth.

I beseech Thee, O Lord, what utility is there in the condemnation of so many thousands of men ? Hell is filled up. The Church is daily depleted. Arise ! Wherefore sleepest Thou, O Lord ? Arise ! and cast not away at the last. Do favourably in Thy good pleasure unto Zion, That The Walls Of Jerusalem May Be Builded.

What is Jerusalem, which is interpreted Vision of Peace, except the Holy City of the Blessed, which is our Mother ? Her walls fell when Lucifer with his angels fell ; in place of whom just men are being received. Therefore, O Lord, do favourably unto Zion, and quickly make up the number of the elect ; and the walls of Jerusalem shall be built and perfected out of new stones, which shall ever give Thee praise, and endure for ever.

*" Then shalt Thou accept the sacrifice of righteous-
ness, the oblations, and the burnt offerings :
then shall they offer young bullocks upon Thine
altar."*

Then, when Thou hast done favourably in Thy
good pleasure unto Zion, shalt Thou accept the
sacrifice of righteousness. Thou shalt accept it,
I say, because Thou shalt consume it with the fire
of Thy love. For thus didst Thou accept the
sacrifice of Moses, and the sacrifice of Elias. For
thus Thou acceptest the sacrifices of righteousness, when Thou bindest with Thy grace the
souls which are content to live justly.

What availeth it to offer Thee sacrifices, when
Thou acceptest them not ?

O Lord, how many sacrifices we daily offer
Thee, which are not pleasing unto Thee, but
rather abominable ! For we offer Thee sacrifices,
not of righteousness, but of our own formalism.
Hence, they are not acceptable unto Thee.

Where now is the glory of the Apostles ?
Where the constancy of the Martyrs ? Where

the fruits of the Preachers ? Where the holy
simplicity of the Monks ? Where the virtues
and good works of the first Christians ?

For then Thou acceptedst their sacrifices
when Thou adornedst them with Thy grace and
virtues. If, likewise, Thou shouldest do favourably unto Zion in Thy good pleasure; then Thou
shalt accept the sacrifice of righteousness ; because the people will begin to live rightly : and
to observe Thy commandments ; and to do justly ;
and Thy benediction will be upon them.

Then the oblations of the priests and of the
clergy shall be acceptable unto Thee ; because,
worldly things forsaken, they shall make themselves ready for the better life ; and the unction
of Thy benediction will be upon their heads.

Then shall be pleasing unto Thee the burnt
offerings of the religious, who, having forsaken
the body, and thrown off lukewarmness, shall be
perfected in every part with the fire of divine love.

Then Bishops and Preachers shall offer young
bullocks upon Thine altar ; because, being perfected in all virtue, and filled with the Holy
Ghost, they shall not hesitate to offer their own
souls for the sake of their flocks.

For what is Thine Altar but Thy Cross, O
Good Jesus, upon which Thou hast been offered ?

What does the sportive young bullock signify, except our flesh ?

Therefore, then, shall they offer young bullocks upon Thine altar, when they offer their bodies upon the Cross, that is, to torture and to death for Thy Name's sake. Then shall the Church flourish. Then shall she enlarge her borders. Then Thy praise shall resound from the ends of the earth. Then joy and gladness shall possess the whole world. Then shall the saints in glory exult : they shall rejoice in their beds, beholding us in the land of the living.

Make, I beseech Thee, O Lord, for me a present *Now* of that *Then*: that Thou mayest have pity on me according to Thy great mercy ; that Thou mayest support me in the sacrifice of righteousness ; in the oblation of holiness ; in the burnt offering of a religious life ; and in the blood-offering of Thy Cross, through which I may be worthy to pass over from this vale of misery, unto that glory, which Thou hast prepared for them that love Thee.

Thanks be to God. Amen.

www.ingramcontent.com/pod-product-compliance
Lightning Source LLC
Chambersburg PA
CBHW022142090426
42742CB00010B/1356